Biomes on Planet Earth

TUNDRA BIOME

Kerri Mazzarella

Table of Contents

A Starfish Book

SEAHORSE PUBLISHING

Teaching Tips for Caregivers:

As a caregiver, you can help your child succeed in school by giving them a strong foundation in language and literacy skills and a desire to learn to read.

This book helps children grow by letting them practice reading skills.

Reading for pleasure and interest will help your child to develop reading skills and will give your child the opportunity to practice these skills in meaningful ways.

- Encourage your child to read on her own at home
- Encourage your child to practice reading aloud
- Encourage activities that require reading
- Establish a reading time
- Talk with your child
- Give your child writing materials

Teaching Tips for Teachers:

Research shows that one of the best ways for students to learn a new topic is to read about it.

Before Reading

- Read the "Words to Know" and discuss the meaning of each word.
- Read the back cover to see what the book is about.

During Reading

- When a student gets to a word that is unknown, ask them to look at the rest of the sentence to find clues to help with the meaning of the unknown word.
- Ask the student to write down any pages of the book that were confusing to them.

After Reading

- Discuss the main idea of the book.
- Ask students to give one detail that they learned in the book by showing a text dependent answer from the book.

TUNDRA BIOME

Earth has many kinds of areas that support life. These are called **biomes**.

Each biome has similar weather patterns, plants, and animals.

What is it like inside a tundra biome?

It is dry, windy, and very cold.

The soil has a layer of **permafrost**.

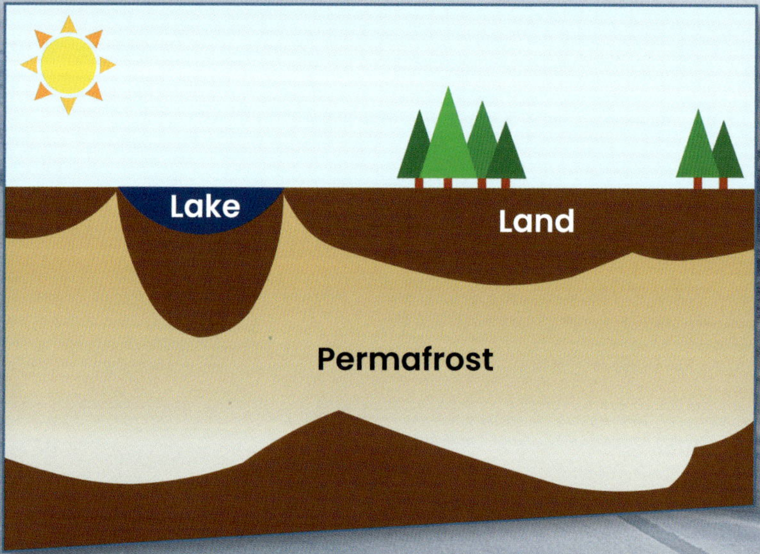

DID YOU KNOW?

The tundra biome includes the Arctic and Antarctica.

Freezing winters last eight months of the year.

Cool summers last about four months.

DID YOU KNOW?

During part of winter, day and night are both dark. The moon's reflection is the only light.

Humans have lived here for thousands of years.

Members of the Aleut and Inuit tribes live here.

The tundra has fish, oil, gas, and other resources people need.

Living things struggle to survive in the tundra.

Small plants have shallow roots.

Some animals **migrate** to warmer places for the winter.

Some **hibernate**.

Algae and **fungi** growing together make lichens.

Lichens cover rocks and soil.

DID YOU KNOW?

Lichens are an important food for caribou, lemmings, and other tundra animals.

Penguins travel over ice.

As they waddle, they carry **nutrients** from sea to land.

An Arctic fox buries food under the snow.

A hungry raven might steal it.

DID YOU KNOW?

The fur of Arctic foxes and other tundra animals turns white in winter. This helps them hide in snow.

All living things in the tundra biome work together for survival.

DID YOU KNOW?

It is easy to find food during tundra summers. Birds, whales, and other animals come to feed.

The tundra biome is important for our planet.

How will you help protect it?

Words to Know

biomes (BYE-ohmz): large areas of similar ecosystems that share weather patterns, rainfall amounts, and types of plants and animals

fungi (FUHN-gye): plant-like organisms that live by decomposing and absorbing the organic material in which they grow; mushrooms are fungi

hibernate (HYE-bur-nate): to sleep for the entire winter because of the cold and because food is hard to find

migrate (MYE-grate): to move to another area or climate at a particular time of the year

nutrients (NOO-tree-uhnts): materials, such as minerals or vitamins, which are needed for healthy growth

permafrost (PUR-muh-frawst): ground that is permanently frozen

Index

Comprehension Questions

1. How many months is winter in the tundra?

a. four
b. eight
c. twelve

2. Lichens are an important ______.

a. rock
b. animal
c. food

3. Some tundra animals turn _____ in winter.

a. warm
b. white
c. brown

4. **True or false:** The tundra is wet and windy.

5. **True or false:** Tundra animals struggle to survive.

Answers

1. b 2. c 3. b 4. False 5. True

About the Author

Kerri Mazzarella was born in New Hampshire and raised in South Florida. She graduated college from Florida State University. After college she worked in the school system as a Speech Language Pathologist. She has a love for children and is passionate about literacy and learning. She lives in South Florida with her husband, Chris. She has four children, and two dogs. They enjoy family time outside and love to travel.

Written by: Kerri Mazzarella
Design by: Kathy Walsh
Editor: Kim Thompson

Library of Congress PCN Data
Tundra Biome / Kerri Mazzarella
Biomes on Planet Earth
ISBN 978-1-63897-469-7 (hard cover)
ISBN 978-1-63897-584-7 (paperback)
ISBN 978-1-63897-699-8 (EPUB)
ISBN 978-1-63897-814-5 (eBook)
Library of Congress Control Number: 2021953361

Printed in the United States of America.

Photographs/Shutterstock: Cover & TOC: ©ANTSTUDIO, © Martin Capek, ©Yeshe-la; Pg 5, 7, 13, 16, 20: ©GraphicStore; Pg 3-21: ©Yeshe-la; Pg 3: ©Galyna Andrushko; Pg 4: ©Dimitrios Karamitros, ©Andrei Stepanov; Pg 6: ©Andrei Stepanov; Pg 8: ©evgenii mitroshin, ©Vladimir Melnikov; Pg 10: ©longtaildog; Pg 11: ©Volodymyr Burdiak, ©Nick Pecker; Pg 12: ©Ksenya_89; Pg 13: ©Nick Pecker; Pg 14: ©steve estvanik; Pg 16: ©NOUREDDINE SIBTI; Pg 17: ©Robert L. Sanson; Pg 18: ©Pav-Pro Photography Ltd; Pg 19: ©longtaildog; Pg 20: ©Scalia Media

Seahorse Publishing Company
www.seahorsepub.com

Published in the United States
Seahorse Publishing
PO Box 771325
Coral Springs, FL 33077

SEAHORSE PUBLISHING